IF
GERMAN
SHEPHERDS
WERE THE ANSWER

A Personal Guide for
Life Experiences and **Sales**

MICHAEL FINALDI

authorHOUSE

AuthorHouse™
1663 Liberty Drive
Bloomington, IN 47403
www.authorhouse.com
Phone: 1 (800) 839-8640

Published by AuthorHouse 01/30/2020

ISBN: 978-1-7283-4327-3 (sc)
ISBN: 978-1-7283-4337-2 (e)

Library of Congress Control Number: 2020901301

Print information available on the last page.

Any people depicted in stock imagery provided by Getty Images are models, and such images are being used for illustrative purposes only. Certain stock imagery © Getty Images.

This book is printed on acid-free paper.

Because of the dynamic nature of the Internet, any web addresses or links contained in this book may have changed since publication and may no longer be valid. The views expressed in this work are solely those of the author and do not necessarily reflect the views of the publisher, and the publisher hereby disclaims any responsibility for them.

Foreword

When I was a little boy growing up in Newark, I always had this persistent fantasy that I would be the king of a small island. Ruling well and being benevolent to the people. A very capable ruler, always fair and peaceful. A beautiful existence. Something that was given to me from up above. Something I felt that I was very capable of doing. Being a good ruler.

So as my life progressed with the twists and turns that we all go through, it seems to me that all the serious decisions I made, that were not easy, somehow brought me to my small island, that being my company Tele-solutions Inc.

I knew from day one that this was for me. I loved the challenge. I loved the hiring and firing. I loved the winning through sales. I looked at competition as a war that had to be won. I wanted Tele to be better than anyone else. I wanted the best for me, my employees, my customers, my country. I believed that by my selling better communication systems, that I would help improve the GNP (Gross National Product). I believed in myself, my judgements, my goals. I was a benevolent owner who had a will to win that would not be denied.

So, in this book, which my son Vincent asked me to write a year ago, I tried to recap some of the stories and share them with my family, my friends, and anyone who can benefit from these experiences. Lastly, my wife Lorraine understood my passion for Tele and success. She was a great homemaker for me and my sons Damon and Vincent and my daughter Cara. She took care of all the important things at home to allow me to not be distracted in any way so I could put 100 percent effort in my goal to be successful. Without her effort and competence, I could not have done it. Lorraine and I have a great partnership. I thank her for that.

So, sit back and read my stories and sayings that I hope will make you successful in business and life.

Introduction

Sales isn't easy. There, I said it. If it were easy, everyone would be doing it. I once had to tell a potential customer just that.

At the beginning of my career, I worked for Bell Tel, a monopoly. So at that point, sales was easy. What choice did people have? But I knew better. If I wanted to leave "Ma Bell," a guaranteed lifetime job, I had to prove to myself that I could sell. So after work at 5 p.m., I got a part-time job selling burglar alarm systems. I knew the hard part was getting **the appointment**.

After making call after call (cold calling, which is really tough), I was struggling. But I didn't give up. Then it happened.

An older lady answered the phone. After my intro, I asked her for the appointment.

Her snitty response was, "Young man, I have two German Shepherds."

I replied, "Lady, if German Shepherds were the answer, I'd be selling German Shepherds."

I knew at that moment I could do this.

That's the point behind this whole book. Sales isn't just

about providing a quick fix to a problem. There's so much that goes into making a sale. You have to know your customer, know your product, know what your customer needs and learn what is the one thing the customer needs most that will get them to buy from you. Buying from you is a key point. What do you have to offer that no one else has? It's not just a product. There's much, much more to it than that. And that's what we are going to explore throughout this book.

***

So why am I writing this book? For a long time, I wondered that myself. Why would anyone want to hear about what I have to say? I mean, I've had a pretty good career, and know a thing or two about sales, but still…

My first thought when I started on this book was to leave it as a legacy for my family. I have a wife, three children, and eight grandchildren (and counting). I built a company that my children are now running. God willing, I'll see my grandchildren take it over some day.

As I thought about the book more, I thought, gee, maybe there are some nuggets of information that I can give out that people might be able to use in their sales career, or even starting up and successfully running a business. God knows I made some mistakes amongst all those successes, and I think learning about them can be helpful as well.

Okay, so I decided the book would be a guide to business and sales. But there was still that whole family legacy thing. Let's face it, I'm not going to be around forever, and I'm sure the Finaldi family will continue on long after I'm gone.

I want those family members to know something about me, even if they won't be able to meet me.

So memoir or sales book? That became the question. At first, the two seemed to be completely at odds. But then I thought about it further, and I realized that that maybe the two could work together. Because so much of what I learned early in my life I took into my sales career with me. Tenacity, dealing with rejection, closing the deal, going with your gut...the list goes on and on.

What I finally came up with, and you're going to see here, is something of a hybrid: stories of my life mixed with career advice, and how those life experiences helped my career. It will be a back and forth, so bear with me. Keep reading, and you'll see how my early life influenced my career, and how the things I learned as a kid growing up in Newark and Union, NJ, stayed with me and helped me persevere in the wild and crazy world of sales.

The Early Me

I was born in Newark, NJ. You may hear the name of that town now and think I must have been a hardened criminal by the age of 10. Not exactly. Newark was different when I grew up than it is now. It wasn't suburbia by any means, but it wasn't the high-crime town it is now. But before we get into more about me, let me take you back and tell you where I came from.

My mother Angelina (Angela) Limongelli was a go-getter. She was the youngest of eight siblings. My father Otto (Otavio) Finaldi, was one of 2. Vito Limongelli was my grandfather, Caroline was my grandmother on my mother's side.. Michael John Finaldi was my grandfather on my father's side. He was very refined and quiet. Frances was my father's mother. The Finaldi side was more aristocratic, but also very refined.

All of my family gave me a lot of strength as a kid, especially being an only child. I felt very secure. They showed me their love. I felt like I could take on the big bad world and win. My family gave me foundation.

Without family it's possible to succeed, but it's not as likely. Every week I got that sense of family love. We always followed the tradition of Sunday family dinners—every weekend. We divided up between Finaldis and Limongellis. I had unconditional love with rules and discipline.

My mother was a seamstress. She was paid by the piece. As I got older, she would have neighbors look after me while she was working, which I didn't like. Then she got her hairdressing license. She worked for someone else for a while, then she opened her own beauty shop. My mother could light up a room when she wanted to. She was a bit of a bullshitter. She was the entrepreneur in the family. I guess I know where I got it from!

My father was absolutely salt of the earth. He worked for Railway Express. He started off loading trucks, but he was smart so they moved him into office to do books. He was steady, the strong silent type. Between the two of them, they gave me a good balance.

My mother was against me working in sales on a draw against commission. She saw how hard it was, and she thought there would be too much pressure. She didn't want me to go out on my own. In fact, she was very negative about it.

My mother was my first lesson in sales psychology. She

taught me to stay away from SNIOPs (susceptible to the negative influence of people).

I told my mother that if she continued to bring me down about leaving Bell that I wouldn't have dinner with her on Sundays until after I left. Once she saw how determined I was, she jumped on my bandwagon. What an about-face that was! Like I said, she really loved me.

My father used to be negative with me when I was young, maybe because of his own inferiority complex. He was very critical of me. Particularly in the way I dressed, because I wanted to look the best I could. That was important to me. I believe the way you look is an expression of the way you feel.

He would approach me in a negative way. He really tried the whole negative inspiration school of thought. My father was neutral about my job until I decided to go on my own completely and open up my own business. He said to me, "Michael, I never really did too much in my life." When he heard the stories of what other employers wanted to offer me for my selling prowess, he said, go ahead, open your own company. You might as well do it on your own. It took him some time, but he got it after a while.

That really helped me have the strength to follow my gut. Remember, he was my father, and fathers have a tremendous influence on their children.

My parents continued to play a big role in mine, my wife's and my kids' lives. Every holiday they would come and stay with us. They would babysit the kids. They would be there for graduations, and all those other big moments. They were there for us all the way.

I am an only child. I know I used to ask why other families had lots of kids and ours only had one, but that was the way it was. My parents never gave me a reasonable explanation for that. Once when I asked, my mother told me that God decides how many children families have. So in my five-year-old mind, I decided that God was unfair. Obviously, today I feel much differently than I did when I was five.

Because I had no siblings, my friends became my extended family, and they were super important to me. They were absolutely the most important people in my life. I was with my friends constantly. We hung out at school, outside of school, all summer…you get the point. They were always there for me and I was there for them.

These guys were cool and fun to be with. They were the ones everyone in school looked up to. When they walked into a room, it was like the parting of the Red Sea. People made room for these guys to come through. Girls loved them. And they were my friends, my crowd. We weren't afraid of anything or anyone, yet we respected law and order.

We played all kinds of competitive games. Growing up in Newark/Union, we would play sports games every minute. And the best part of it was, in my opinion, that parents were not involved at all. It wasn't part of the life. They stayed inside and did whatever it was they did, and we were outside, unless the weather was really extreme.

Here's how we did it: The two best players were captains, and they would pick their teams. We would flip for first pick and then choose our team We tried to balance teams by ability. That way, no one's egos were bruised. And if you cared about being the first pick you had to get better at what you did.

All my life I condemned myself for not going out for high school sports. But looking back now, I did play sports; it was very competitive. It just wasn't formal. If I had to do it all over again, I would have gotten as involved as possible in high school sports/activities. I feel now like I missed out on a lot of the high school experience and certainly the friendships and relationships that could have grown from those experiences.

What I see now is that parents are too heavily involved in their children's activities. No one can just be a kid anymore and have fun without parental intervention or rules or umpires. In my day, kids would settle disputes their own way. We learned life lessons that way. I think there should be a little more freedom and let kids play.

That's not to say that parents shouldn't coach their kids. It can be a great bonding experience for a parent to coach their kids and help them learn a game or activity. The problem I see is when parents become "too" involved, and play their kids above others, even if the talent isn't there. It's the kids' game. Let them play it and have fun—and learn to compete!

At this point in my life, I was a "lonely only," but I was living in the city with 30 kids on each block, three-family houses, three feet separated each house, it wasn't so bad. I had my lifetime friends, and they made up for not having my own brothers and sisters.

Or so I thought.

Everyone has a turning point in their life, a time when they find their inner strength. Mine came when I was 13 years old.

One day, I'm in the middle of eighth grade, my parents sit me down and tell me, "we bought a house in Union."

Union? Really? It was only five miles away from Newark, but it might as well have been 500 miles. I didn't drive, and there were no cell phones or text messages back then. My parents were ripping me away from the only friends I'd ever known, the people I really cared about.

I didn't understand it. Why would they do this to me? They explained that it was a house instead of an apartment, and it was a safer place, all that stuff. But none of it meant anything to me. All I could see was that I was leaving my friends, my people, the guys who were there for me from the very beginning.

That's when I found my inner strength. I couldn't understand why my parents would do this, but I didn't have a choice. I ended up going to Union High School, and I rarely saw the guys I grew up with.

Funny thing is, my parents never told me, at least at the time, why they chose to do that. Why would they move me away from everything I'd ever known at such a pivotal time in my life, at an age where friends are the most important things you have?

What it really came down to was economic gain for them. They were "moving on up" to suburbia. They finally got to have the one-family house with a garage and a yard that they'd always dreamed about.

Now as a grown man, I can understand their desire

to have this. Every man wants to provide a home for his family.

The problem, from my standpoint, was not the how, but the when. Why couldn't they have let me finish high school with all the friends I'd known my whole life?

Years later, they finally told me that part of their thinking was that they thought I was getting too "enamored with the wise guys." Don't forget, this was an Italian neighborhood in Newark. Were the guys I hung out with getting in trouble? Not when we were kids, no. Have they gotten in trouble since then? Absolutely. Some of them have become permanent guests of the state by now.

Would I have committed a crime? I'd like to say no, but at this point in my life, I can see why my parents made the decision to move me away from them. The power was pretty tempting. That wasn't a life they wanted for me, or, as an adult, that I would want for myself.

Still, it was a big pivotal point in my formative years. It was a huge change that was thrust upon me, not one I necessarily wanted or went looking for. I had to take that change and make the best of it. I believe I did that.

When I lived in Newark, I had also gone to Catholic school. When we moved to Union, my parents gave me the choice to go to Catholic or public school. I chose public, and that was a mistake. I walked into school in the middle of eighth grade not knowing anyone. It wasn't a good feeling.

However, it didn't take me long to get a reputation. One day I saw a kid bullying a kid in the school who was slightly retarded. I got upset. I knew no real tough guy would pick on a kid like this. So what did I do? I beat up the bully.

As I was watching this scenario unfold in the hallway, on my second day of school in Union, I said to the kid next to me, "Who is this kid?" He replied, "That's so-and-so. He's one of the tough kids." I said, "Watch this."

I went up to the kid and said, "Hey, jerk, why are you picking on someone who is mentally challenged? Why don't you try picking on me?" We met after school, off school grounds, and I gave him a good beating. Like I said, getting a reputation didn't take me long.

But still, I was 13 years old, living in Unionville, NJ, which was a farmland back in 1960. I was very depressed. I was alone.

. . . .

I remember another time when I was walking home from school with my books in my arms. There were three kids sitting on their porch. One of them yelled from the porch, "Hey, is your name Michael?" I responded yes.

"Your mom called our mom and asked if we would play with you." The tone was completely mocking. I was totally embarrassed and felt ridiculed and disrespected.

So what did I do? I threw my books down on the ground and challenged the three to come off the porch and fight. In those days, we did that. But not one of them took my challenge. A few days later I saw one of the three alone on his bike delivering newspapers. I grabbed the handlebars with both my hands so he couldn't ride away and said, "Remember me? My name is Michael, and my mom asked if you would play with me. Well how about playing with me now? Get off the bike."

As I menacingly stared him down, he profusely apologized. "It wasn't me," he said. I made my first friend in Unionville.

I was pretty mad at my mom for that one. I actually told her not to do that, to interfere with my life. She'd messed things up enough by taking me away from all my friends. Now she was trying to make new ones for me? That wasn't going to fly with a teenager. We didn't talk for a little while over that one.

Another mistake I made in high school was not trying out for any sports teams. I was pretty hung up about my height back then. I let a lot of life pass me by in high school because I didn't think I'd be good enough since I wasn't big enough. I even remember the high school wrestling coach telling me not to let my height bother me.

"Don't worry about size. It's what God gave you," he said. "Don't let it be a determining factor." I wish I'd listened. I guess back then one of my biggest fears was losing or being rejected or feeling inadequate. Hmmm…seems that's a big fear in the world of sales, too, isn't it? More on that later.

Hearing no isn't fun, there's no doubt about that. I remember one year I tried out for the Little League team, and I actually made it. Hundreds of kids tried out, and only 15-18 kids made it. And I was one of them. They told me I was going to play second base, and they told all of us to go to a certain sporting goods store in town and pick up our uniforms.

I got there early to pick up my uniform, and as I came

in, I saw another kid's dad talking to the Little League coach. When they were finished talking, I went up to the coach and asked for my uniform. The coach looked at me and said, "What is your name?"

I answered, "Michael Finaldi."

He said, "I'm sorry, Michael, but you didn't make the team after all."

I later found out that the coach gave my spot to the kid whose father I saw in the store earlier that day.

That was one of my first experiences with learning that not everybody plays fair to get what they want. Seems like another sales lesson to be learned there, yes?

. . . .

CHAPTER
2

College And The Draft
(And No, I Don't Mean Sports)

After my less-than-stellar experience in high school, I had to figure out what to do with the rest of my life. College wasn't a must back then like it is today. Not everyone went to college. Not everyone was cut out for it. But my parents always told me, "You're going to college." When I grew up in Newark and Union, grades weren't important to me or a lot of the kids my age. I didn't give college much thought at all. In fact, I didn't consider college until April of my senior year. That's how detached I was from it. All I cared about was passing. No one told me I should work hard to get good grades or why I should do that. No one ever said that if you don't get good grades you can't go to whatever school you want. I was young and I didn't get it, and no one connected the dots for me.

So now it's April of my senior year and reality is hitting me. Low SAT scores, low grades, no choice of schools and parents telling me I had to go to college. My guidance counselor told me about this school, Windham College in Vermont. It wasn't accredited at the time, but it was close to home. I remember thinking, how far is Vermont from New Jersey? Only three and a half hours. Okay, it was drivable. I could get home pretty easily on weekends.

So I ended up at Windham, and it wasn't the best choice for me. Windham was a liberal school. I wasn't avant garde, like many of my peers were. I wasn't mad at the world, which seemed to be the norm at that time. I listened to Frank Sinatra, The Four Seasons, Dion, and The Beach Boys. I liked a scotch and soda and beautiful, color-coordinated clothes. Looking good made me feel good. I wasn't like the other kids in college back then. Remember, you dress the way you think and feel. I guess I thought and felt much differently than my peers did.

I didn't do well at college. I was just 17 years old, and away from home for the first time, in a foreign land called Vermont. I just didn't fit there. I was so depressed that all I did was go to class, come back to my dorm, and go to sleep. I didn't go to school with any of my friends. I was on my own and not ready for it.

But did I quit? I did not. It wasn't in my DNA. I knew I needed a degree for my future life as a businessman.

I went on academic probation in the first semester of freshman year. I came home for Christmas break, and in my second semester I did just enough to come off probation. I also did more to look the part of the hippie college kid.

My sophomore year was a real disaster. I had a terrible GPA. I had already taken a summer class after freshman year. I told my parents, "I'm not college material. I'm wasting your money." They said, "It's our money, and we will decide how to spend it. We will ask you for one more semester. If you do badly, we're done."

At this point I'm 19, and I'm calling myself a man. Now I figure I should start studying because it's my junior year, and I only cared about getting a degree. College was a means to an end. I got my own apartment in junior year. Suddenly, I flourished. I ended up with a Bachelor of Arts in Economics. My real love was psychology, because that's about people, and that's what I really liked and still do today. I already knew it was the secret to life and what motivates people to do what they do. But I didn't want to change majors, so I got a psychology minor.

I graduated Windham in 1969. I was so proud. I had accomplished my first task as a future businessman and entrepreneur. And I didn't give up. That's the key.

By this time, though, Viet Nam was in the forefront, and I was classified 1A. Any 1A male was going to be drafted. It was a foregone conclusion.

My parents loved me so much that when they knew I would be drafted they offered to leave New Jersey and the United States for Canada. They offered to give up everything they had, everything they'd worked for, to move to Canada so I wouldn't have to go to war. And at that time, there was no clemency. If they moved to Canada, they would have to stay there for the rest of their lives.

But I wasn't selfish. I wouldn't do that to them. Everything they had was here—their lives, their family, their friends, their jobs. I couldn't take all that away from them. So I trusted God and fate to take me through this.

One morning, about two weeks after I graduated college, my mother came into my room at 7 a.m., ripped the covers off, and said, "okay, you've been home now, you've been having fun, now it's time to get a job."

I told her there was no way anyone was going to hire me. I was 1A for the draft. There was no way I was going to get out of getting drafted. Who would hire me under those circumstances?

But my mother insisted. She told me I had to be out of the house by 9 every morning, and I wasn't allowed to come back in until 5 at night. So what did I do? Not much. I sat outside my house. There was nowhere to go! I knew I wasn't going to be able to get a job, so what was I supposed to do?

Finally, I sat down and made a deal with my parents. I said, "This is ridiculous. I know I'm going to get drafted."

Still, they made me do something, so I ended up going to real estate school. Around the same time, I put my name on the waiting list for the National Guard, hoping I would get called before I got drafted. No sooner did I finish school than I got drafted.

I had a cousin in the guard. He was able to get me in, and on August 12, 1969, I was sworn into National Guard in Elizabeth. I was part of the 50th armor division. The next day, August 13, 1969, I got drafted. Since I'd already been sworn in to the guard, I didn't have to go to war.

My next stop was Fort Bragg, NC, home of the "Airborne Rangers." My first time on an airplane was in November of 1969. I was 21 years old.

I served six months in the guard. I was a helicopter repair parts specialist. I went to Fort Lee, Virginia for advanced infantry training in my trade. I finish my tour of six months, then came home. I spent 5.5 years as a NJ National Guard, so today I'm considered a veteran.

My time in the guard taught me a lot that helped my sales and leadership career along.

First thing I learned is that it pays to be friendly with people. Because of my outgoing demeanor, I was chatting with an older recruit when we were both in the latrine. The next thing I know, the Army made me a squad leader with Sergeant stripes on my shoulder. I led seven soldiers in the daily duties that were required. I liked being a leader. It felt right to me.

My first challenge as a squad leader came from a tough Southern boy from Georgia. My squad was assigned to clean the bathrooms. I broke down each part of the cleaning for my squad. The Georgia boy refused to do anything. Everyone was pulling their weight except him. And they were all watching me to see what I would do and he repeated, "I'm not cleaning anything."

I knew I had a choice. I could step down right then, go complain to the brass, or confront him head on. If I left my temporary sergeant stripes on my arm, he could be court marshalled if we fought. I decided to take off the stripes. I removed them from my arm and challenged him to a fight.

It was a draw but a big win for me. By standing up for my integrity, I won over my squad and the Georgia recruit became my best soldier.

Was being a leader in my future? It's certainly starting to look that way.

What's the takeaway? Always do the right thing and you can't lose.

. . . .

CHAPTER

3

Real Life Awaits

Now it's April of 1970, and I have to get a real job. Real estate? I loved it, but there was a problem. I was 22 and single, and I liked weekends. In real estate, all of the work comes on weekends. I'd only gone to real estate school as a bargain with my parents, The only jobs I would ever consider were sales. I started looking for sales jobs.

One of the first things I did, though, was to get my own apartment. I got a studio apartment in Maplewood when I was 22.

I told my parents about moving out at dinner one night. Of course, the first thing they thought was that they did something wrong. They told me they'd let me use the living room to entertain, and they'd go upstairs if I wanted to have people over.

I told them that this wasn't about us. It was about me, and how it was time for me to be a man.

You can't be a man living at home in mommy and daddy's house. If you're saving to buy something for a few months, that's fine. But after that, get out. It's time.

I remember the first night in my apartment, as I went in there with old curtains, hardly a tv working, a studio bed, it was pretty stark. That first night, I thought, what the hell am I doing here? I had the luxury of home and I gave that up? I'm living alone. But that lasted one night.

The moral here is that for my business life to expand, I needed my personal life to expand. It made me feel good about myself.

. . . .

At that point, I was evaluating what I wanted to do with my life and what I liked to do and what I did well. I realized that I was a jack of all trades and a master of none. But I took notice of one thing, and that was that I always seemed to win any silly game I played, like ping pong or pool. Not that I was that much better than everyone else, but I wanted to win more than anyone else. I was ultra-competitive. I wanted to win. Period. One rule I had, though, was no cheating. That wasn't winning.

My job hunt was fruitful. I get into NJ Bell as a salesman, which was the highest level non-management position. I was also offered a job at Mobile Chemical in Edison. Competitive offers! Wasn't this fun! So why did I choose Bell? For the women, of course. Remember, I was 22. And I did want to get married someday. There were more women at Bell than at Mobile. That decision ended up hurting me.

At Bell, people got promoted about 12 – 18 months. You had to compete with 30-50 people. Every year, about 12-15 got promoted. So, I go two years, no promotion. Three years, no promotion. Now I'm thinking, I gotta do something about this.

They'd have sales contests at Bell. I won all the sales contests. I still didn't get promoted. At the biggest sales contest of the year, I decide I'm going to do double what the next person did. I did that. And I STILL didn't get promoted.

In outside sales at Bell, they had a one-time sales contest for a new product. They posted the names on the wall for everyone to see who was selling the most systems. I had won all the sales contests they had prior to this one. I said to myself, not only will I win this, but I will double the next guy's results. There would be no doubt or question as to who would get the next promotion. This surely would end my frustration about not being promoted.

I did double the next guy's results. It was remarkable. A manager rode with me to find out how I did it. Managers at Bell Tel never really understood sales. They were a monopoly, remember? People didn't have a choice.

I sold more because of desire, personality, and knowledge of my products and the decision makers and their businesses. And people liked me! It was easy for me, like putting a knife through butter. I might have been born for this!

During this time when I couldn't get promoted, there was a job called Inside Telephone Demand. It was stringent and difficult. You had to answer all business calls from all of Union County. Normally they assigned you this only for six months. You were on the phone all day every day nonstop from 9-5, and I guess they figured that was enough for anyone. I did it for two years. They wanted to break me. They wanted me to quit. I became so good at it that I didn't need the books anymore. I was orchestrating.

And I STILL didn't get promoted.

It became increasingly embarrassing for me. Month in and month out, year in and year out. Usually on a Friday afternoon the sales managers would call a meeting with all 50 salespeople holding their breath to see who would get the next promotion. We'd all be sitting on the edge of our seats in anticipation, hoping they would call our name. After they made the announcement, everyone would then clap, and your career at Bell would take off. It was the only path to more income, more respectability, a better career path. The promotion to Communication Consultant (CC) was paramount in my mind.

. . . .

Month after month, year after year, they would announce the names of all of my peers but never mine. I would then congratulate my associate, knowing that I was the better salesman. It started to get too hard for me to show happiness for them. I would get too choked up trying to congratulate them.

One day, after I won the big sales contest by doubling

my nearest competitor, my manager at Bell said to me, "Finaldi, I have a question for you. We have noticed you're different. Are you willing to pay the price?" He left me with those words and my thoughts. I didn't know how to take it.

I walked away conflicted. I liked the thought of being different, but he spun it in a negative way. I did dress better than most. My cars were used luxury cars rather than new and modest. My body language was confident, positive, and open. I liked myself and other people. This attitude must have bothered them. Then I realized, after thinking about it, it was time for me to move on. But I had to settle something first.

After waiting and waiting for the promotion that wouldn't come, now what do I do? Complain about the injustice? Wallow in my own self-pity? Shrink back into mediocrity? NO. Never. I decided to leave Bell for sure, but with a little twist.

Bell allowed disgruntled employees to challenge the system by going to one's immediate manager formally in writing to ask to go up the ladder to prove if there was an injustice committed. That's exactly what I did.

I had decided ahead of my actions to leave Bell. I said to myself and my wife Lorraine that even if they offered me the presidency of Bell Tel, I would not change my mind.

....

So up the ladder I went until finally I got to the head guy's office in Woodbridge. I walked in and he was looking at my file. He knew why I was there and made some comments to me.

"You have won all the sales contests we've ever had, and you have been labeled as promotable now in our internal records. Lastly you have missed one day of work in five years!"

"I was really sick that day," I answered.

He shook his head, seeming perplexed. He asked me to come back to his office the next day at 10. I did. I sat in his office, just the two of us. Then another man, my immediate sales manager, walked in. He looked at me and wondered what I was doing there with the big boss. The big boss asked my manager why I hadn't been promoted. His answer shocked me.

"As long as Mike Finaldi works for me, he will never be promoted." I didn't know in that moment if I wanted to cry or fight. I was blindsided. It was very emotional. The big boss told the manager to leave immediately. I just sat there, stunned. He tried to console me by telling me that an injustice had been done to me, that the sales manager would be transferred to a desk far away from salespeople, and that I would be promoted as soon as possible.

I took a deep breath and said, "Thank you, but I have something I want to say.

"First, I did this for two reasons. The first was to find out why I'm not being promoted. Now I know. But also, just as important, I did not want this to happen to someone else. If by my actions I have helped stop this, then I'm glad I did it.

"The second reason was to give you my resignation from Bell Tel."

"But Mike, you'll have the next promotion, I promise," he said.

"Thank you sincerely, but I don't want it. It's anticlimactic for me now. I'm moving on."

What are the takeaways from this experience? Life can be unfair. Knowing that, deal with it. Trust in God and in yourself. Follow your heart. It's always the right thing to do.

4

Using My Gut

During my Bell years, I was single, so I would go out a lot after work. I met my wife Lorraine on a Thursday night at The Chateau in Union. When I first saw her, something happened in me. It was like I was hit by lightning. I hadn't even said a word to her yet, and it was love at first sight. I went over to her and asked her to dance. I was talking to her, but she was giving me the brush off. I really had to push. I remember telling her, "I want to call you. I really will call. Give me a chance." Then it blossomed into a love affair. About three years later we got married.

We've been good together for many years now. She was a legal secretary with a steady job. When I finally decided to leave Bell to go on commission, I knew we'd have enough for groceries. That helped me psychologically and made it a little easier for me to make the decision.

I have always worked using my gut feelings. It's a good way to work. Your gut never steers you wrong. Deciding to leave Bell was one of the first times I used my gut in a professional sense. I just knew that it wasn't the right place for me anymore, and I wasn't going to advance if I stayed there. It was a gut feeling.

At the time I decided this, I was married, but I didn't have any of my kids yet and Lorraine was still working. Maybe my gut would have told me something different if my circumstances were different, but I knew I was ready to go.

. . . .

I decided to stay in the telephone industry, since that was where all my training was—in telephony. I was going to work with a smaller company. There was more risk, but much better training. I worked for a guy named Norman Moon, president of Garden State Telephone in South Plainfield. He had been with Bell also, as a lineman, and they wouldn't promote him into sales. So, he started his own company, and I worked with him for a draw against commission—that was it. No regular salary. Sounds risky, and it was, but I learned a lot from Norman.

I rode with him on his sales calls every single day for 45 days. I must have asked him a million questions. The information he gave me was crucial to my success.

After that 45 days, Norman asked me if I had any more

sales questions. I answered, no, you taught me well. I've seen everything.

Then he said, "You're ready. Go get 'em, tiger." So off I went. And for the first month, I didn't sell anything.

That's right—NOTHING.

I was beside myself, disappointed, and couldn't figure out why I couldn't sell any systems. I went to Norman and told him that I didn't think I was cut out for selling telephone systems at all. He could have just said okay, goodbye, but he didn't. He asked me to walk him through my whole process. "Tell me everything you do from the moment you walk in the door to the moment you leave," he said.

So I went through the process, and he told me I was doing everything right except for **one thing.**

I WASN'T ASKING FOR THE ORDER.

That's right. I was doing all the right things in my sales calls, but I wasn't closing sales because I wasn't asking for the order! Sounds pretty simple, right? Ask and ye shall receive. Not necessarily.

I was doubting myself. I wasn't sure if the customer was ready to buy when I was finished with my sales presentation. I had to learn to trust myself, and know that I had done everything right, and then actually ask for them to sign on the line.

Once I started doing this, I found that it really worked! I learned what the customer wanted, and then I gradually got to know when it was time to stop pitching and simply ask for the order. This technique got me to stop wasting a lot of time.

It really is pretty simple. Think about it for a second. Let's say you're at a meeting for a potential close, and the person you're meeting with has just been informed that his mother died. You would know not to ask for the order at that moment. You would trust your feelings and you would be correct. If you are a fair and balanced person, you know you can trust your instincts.

That understanding alone was worth millions of dollars to me. What a find! I'd never heard this before from anyone else. It was all mine. In my opinion, it was simple genius. I had a trustworthy formula that I could use every time and in a split second. Just trust your instincts. In fact, this led to a defining moment for me that I put into a working formula: WHEN IN DOUBT, ASK FOR THE ORDER.

....

After my first year with Norman, working out of the main office in South Plainfield, and doing very well selling, he asked me if I'd be interested in opening up a branch office in North Jersey for Garden State Telephone. After giving it some thought, with my aspirations of always wanting to be in charge, I said yes and started looking for a location. I found a great spot in Fairfield, NJ, furnished it, and hired salespeople and a secretary.

Talk about control…Norman had so much faith in me that, surprisingly, he never even came to see the office before we signed the lease.

It was successful immediately. There was no ramping up time. From day one, the office was very profitable. Low overhead (part-time secretary) and big sales. Isn't that always a formula that works?

After five years of this, the industry was booming. This was my own domain—my kingdom, if you will. On Wednesdays, the main office had weekly sales meetings. I drove down to South Plainfield to run the sales meetings for everybody, including my own salesmen from Fairfield. I did it gratis. I felt that if they trusted me with an office, I wanted to give back my time and my talent to run their weekly sales meetings for everyone, even though there was no extra financial compensation for me.

During the late 70s, the telephone industry was really heating up. More and more, the monopoly of AT&T and Ma Bell were being chipped away at. Competitors were starting to come out of the woodwork. I started to get offers to partner up and become a part owner with various competitors in the area.

....

Norman had a competitor, Mr. Wichansky with a company called TCI (Telephone Controls and Installation). He was born with a silver spoon in his mouth and was a winner with a strong sales personality.

However, when competing against Mr. Wichansky, it wasn't a fair fight. If he wanted the account, he would discount any amount, whereas I was limited in what I could offer.

After a while, he was driving me crazy. I would lose more than I would win because of his super discounting. But he respected my sales talents.

So here's what I did. Rather than lose all the time, I'm said to myself, "I'm gonna make Mr. Wichansky sell it for so low that it will hurt him worse than it hurts me to lose the order."

When I would go out to customers, I would ask if they'd been looking, asked if they looked at TCI. I told customers I couldn't compete with him because he gives his equipment away, but I'd like to help them buy from them anyway, but at the lowest price. And I was willing to show the customer how low Mr. Wichansky could go. The customer and I were in cahoots to make him sell at very little profit. Naturally, the customer would be thrilled to be able to do this.

Mr. Wichansky would call me at night at my house. My wife, Lorraine, would be wildly signaling me from the background, saying "why are you talking to him?" He would then ask, "What are you doing to me?" I would reply, "What are you doing to me? I can't compete with you because you give it away. So I'm going to make you give it away at such a low price that by me losing the order, I don't care. I'll make you lose worse. You're competing against me unfairly. This is not a fair fight because of your ownership position. So I'm gonna make you pay the price."

In the meantime, Mr. Wichansky was still asking me what it would take for me to come and work for him. He was offering me anything I could possibly want—cars, trips, expense account, salary plus commission. I kept saying no. He would keep asking, what do you want? I told him I wanted to be an owner in a telephone company. That's when he offered me a one-third interest of a subsidiary that we would call TCI Services. To the world, it looked like one company, but in reality, it was two. I'd be the one-third owner of one, with Mr. Wichansky and his brother owning the other two-thirds. It was 1980, and the telephone industry was booming, but still a monopoly under Bell.

I went back to Norman with this information and suggested that I should get a one-third interest in the Fairfield office. Since I was doing a million in sales per year with very little overhead, I was certainly worth that. We would treat Fairfield as a subsidiary of the main company. I wasn't asking to be a partner in the main company. If he could do that, I'd be his partner for life. Norman said no— he told me it would be too difficult with all the accounting that would need to be done, which was a lame excuse, in my mind. I think Norman eventually realized that if you have a million-dollar salesperson, you don't let him go. There aren't that many around.

Two years later, when I was totally on my own, Norman came to my office with hat in hand. After I left, his company suffered. He didn't just lose my sales numbers, but also my insights, talents, and willingness to help others become successful. My enthusiasm and sales dynamics left with me.

....

He said, "Mike, I made a mistake. Can we partner up again?" I said, "Norman, I thank you for everything you've done for me, especially teaching me to be a professional salesperson. By far, you were my best mentor. But at this point, you have nothing I need. You have nothing to offer me. I'm already a successful telephone company."

Norman walked away sad. He knew he blew it, and even said that to me. He blamed a junior partner and walked away sheepishly and dejected.

The moral of this story? Follow your instincts. Do what's right for you without fear and don't look back. Trust your gut. Starting to sound familiar?

After Norman surprisingly said no to me, and before I ended up with my own company as a solo owner, Mr. Wichansky was still there, still offering me anything my heart desired, including the partnership. I finally told him no, because I wanted to be an owner.

Mr. Wichansky owned a company called TCI in Elizabeth, NJ. He wanted me to work with him. I told him I wanted to be an owner, so he offered me ownership of TCI Services, which would be an offshoot of his main company, TCI. I ended up owning one-third of TCI Services, and he and his brother owned two-thirds of this fledgling company.

However, I made a mistake. I kept insisting to him that I wanted my own office, my own space. I knew I needed that. It was critical. If you share space with a superior, you're not really sharing space. It's his.

....

After I was willing to walk away from the new deal over having my own office space, he finally gave in and agreed to let me find my own space. But at that point, I gave in and said I'd go to his space. I was starting to become practical now. From a dollar standpoint, it seemed to make sense to go to his offices. And that was the mistake. I never should have done it, as you'll soon see. I got away with the mistake, but only through happenstance.

In life, having your own space is probably one of the most critical things to success. In your own private domain, you're not cowtowing to anyone, business or personal.

So now I'm going through the process to get a business up and running—hiring people, buying equipment, training, etc. I'm spending all the money long-term. Little did I know that a company named Intertel was entertaining the idea of buying TCI and TCI Services, as they were making a public offering. Mr. Wichansky neglected—purposely—telling me this until 30 days before the sale was going to happen! Intertel was offering him $2 million in stock based on the public offering. They didn't care how he divided it up. They were paying based on five times earnings. I had very little in earnings because I was building a company long term. So now Mr. Wichansky and his brother were spending little money and showing high earnings, and I had very little to show in the way of earnings.

I went to the lawyer's office on the day of the sale in Newark, NJ. Everyone was represented with their own attorneys, including mine, Saul Zimmerman. One of the big 8 accounting firms was on the phone orchestrating the purchase of TCI and TCI Services, if I agreed to go along with it.

They offered me a two-year deal worth $75,000 per year plus stock options and commissions. I would be their sales manager for the NJ/NY office. They saw I was reluctant, so they upped it to a one-year deal of $125,000 salary, plus stock options that would have brought the deal to about $250,000. I was free to leave after that if I wanted to.

This was a lot of money for me. I asked to be excused, so I could collect my thoughts and say a prayer.

My attorney, Saul, advised me to take the deal. From his point of view, it was a cushy deal for one year. He said, "Mike, take the deal. $250K is a lot of money, especially in 1980. After a year, you can do what you want."

But I wanted to be on my own. I had groomed myself for this moment that happened to fall in my lap through circumstance, for all of my life. If I stayed with Intertel and Mr. Wichansky, I would have lost all of my momentum and worked for them for the rest of my career as their underling.

So I cleared my throat, and said, "I'll pass." Mr. Wichansky said, incredulously, "What did you say?" I said more clearly, "I pass." I just couldn't do it. It was a ballsy move.

When I said that, he jumped up off his seat, and said, "I can't believe…if I lined up 100 men with the offer that was given today to Michael, they would say okay. I find the one in 100 that says no."

His peers and the lawyers scolded him and said, "Mr. Wichansky, sit down. Mr. Finaldi has made his final decision and the Intertel stock transfer will be written accordingly."

After the meeting ended, Saul and I were in the elevator, just the two of us, going down to his office. He looks at me and says, "Mike, as a lawyer, I've seen a lot of things, but today was something special. How do you feel?"

I looked at Saul and said, "Saul, I'm about five feet seven inches tall, and right now I feel like a giant."

He shook his head and said, "Well done, Mike. You followed your heart."

So now I've made this great, gutsy transition to be on my own. But what do I do? Remember, I had no office space.

I sold 100 customers in a year. But my partner Mr. Wichansky owned 66 of them, and I had 33. I kept those 33 under my new company (whatever name that would be), one technician, one secretary, me, and a dream. I was following my heart.

At that point, in 1981, Tele-Solutions was born. I went to incorporate, and every name I wanted was already taken. Saul would incorporate for me. He was actually the one that offered up the name that I immediately fell in love with— Tele-Solutions, Inc. He called me back in 10 minutes and said, "you got it!" It was free. I was on my way to the rest of my career.

I found space on Route 22 in Union and signed a three-year lease—gulp. Tele-Solutions success was instantaneous. The industry was booming. I was selling like crazy, hiring, and continuing to learn to become a successful entrepreneur. I must admit, it came very easily to me.

I signed a new multi-year lease extension at my existing space. However, there was a bar/restaurant up the street on Route 22 called Harper's that had food and drinks. Happy hours on Fridays were always fun. I enjoyed going there and met a realtor, Ron Klaus, there who I became friends with.

I had just signed the new lease on the building when Ron called me one day to tell me that Harper's was for sale.

I told him I probably wouldn't stay married if I bought a nightclub and was not at all interested. But then I began to think about what a great space it was for Tele-Solutions. But remember, I had just signed a new lease. Now what do I do?

After I looked at the building and had a contractor come in and give me some quotes about renovating the space from a bar to offices. I made an offer on the building, but I told the owners of the property that I didn't need their liquor license. I ended up buying the building, a 5,000-square-foot building on an acre of land on Route 22 in Union, for an unbelievable price. I was a wrong-way buyer. No one was competing with me for a bar with a leaky roof and township problems.

. . . .

Use this theory for everything you buy in real estate, if you can. As you've heard many times before, only the location matters, not the building itself. You can always renovate or build new...you can't change the location.

But now, remember, I have this lease on my hands that I'd just signed. I went to see the owner, Mrs. Urban, who was an old biddy. I went with a check in hand, knowing I was breaking a lease, but willing to make it right. I had made friends with the receptionist, who felt sure that Mrs. Urban would make a deal with me.

Well, Mrs. Urban wasn't in the mood to make a deal. She decided she wanted the whole amount. I tried to explain to her that this wouldn't make any sense. Why would I pay her the whole amount up front when I could pay her monthly and do anything I wanted with the space?

She still didn't want to deal. After three times of explaining the situation to her, she was still being unreasonable, so I just left without giving her a check. What else could I do?

On the way out of the office, I explained the bizarre situation to the receptionist, who seemed sympathetic, but didn't say anything. A month later, I happily moved into the new Finaldi building on Route 22, where Tele-Solutions is still located today.

Meanwhile, I'm waiting for legal notice that I was being sued for breaking the lease with Mrs. Urban, especially since the company name remained the same. Weeks, months, years, go by, and still no notice. I didn't understand why. I figured for sure she would try to get me to pay something.

I don't really know what happened. I can only believe that the sympathetic receptionist must have torn up my file. I never heard from Mrs. Urban again.

....

The moral of this story is that I was prepared to do what was right by acknowledging I was breaking my lease. It's the only way to conduct business. As it turns out, I'm still surprised at the way it turned out.

In addition, remember to be nice to everyone, no matter who they are or what their status is. You never know who will help you and how.

....

Michael Finaldi and his extended family

From left: Faye and Damon Finaldi, John
and Cara Miscia, Lisa and Vincent Finaldi,
Lorraine and Michael Finaldi

Lorraine and Michael Finaldi on their wedding day

Michael Finaldi and his golf partners

Cara, Lorraine, Damon, Vincent, and Michael Finaldi

Michael Finaldi and golf partners (yes, that is Mickey Mantle in the middle!)

Michael Finaldi receiving an award

The Tele-Solutions building in Union, NJ

Michael Finaldi with his children,
Cara, Damon, and Vincent

CHAPTER 5

Golf And Business

So here I am, 35 years old, and a fledgling as a business owner, when an accountant takes me out to play golf. I really enjoyed it and took it up as a regular sport. Little did I realize at that time, how much of an impact golf would have on making business deals.

There was a time I went to Kiawa Island in South Carolina to play in a Pro-Am tournament, representing Colonia Country Club in Colonia, NJ, where I ended up playing a guy named Tony Russo, a member of Suburban Country Club in Union, and the owner of Hillside Wire and Cable. He was about 15 years older than I, and a much better golfer than I was. After golf we went in for cocktails, as was typical after a day on the links. Tony asked me what

I did, and I told him about my business and asked him the same. It was a great day out, but I didn't give it any more thought.

About 3-6 months later I get a call from Tony's secretary. "Mr. Russo asked if you would come in to discuss a phone system," she said.

I met with him a couple of times and told him and I had a good solution for him. At the second meeting, I brought a contract with me with pricing.

Tony asked me how much the system was. I told him $50,000. He said great and signed the contract on the spot.

I have one cardinal rule in sales. Once someone commits to giving you an order, ask for deposit, give installation date, then leave. DON'T SAY ANOTHER WORD!

With Tony, however, I broke this sales rule, and I did it by instinct. I told Tony about my rule first. "Tony, I usually say the least I can, and then I like to leave. But I'm going to make an exception for you," I said. "You played golf with me once, you contacted me a few months later to come to your office for your interest in a phone system. You signed my order, didn't talk to any of my competition, didn't question my pricing. You simply signed the order. Why did you do that? Why didn't you shop around?"

Tony said, "Did I play golf with you? I didn't have to learn anymore about you. In golf, everything comes out. You can't hide it. You can't phony your way through golf."

Hmmm…that was interesting. Little did I know how much golf tells you about a person, but Tony was right. You learn a lot about people out on the golf course. I found that to be true many times over in the course of my career. There's an old expression, "if there's any larceny in a man, it will come out in golf." How true that is.

When I first decided to take up the sport, I didn't play golf to get deals, but little did I realize how many deals I could make on the course. The amount of deals through contacts really opened my eyes to the importance of the game. When I joined a country club, I wrote so much business because the people I met and played with were decision makers. What better way to meet those decision makers than on a golf course?

Does that mean you should play golf if you hate it? No, of course not. If you're doing it just to look good, or to try and get a deal, people will see right through you. Remember, you can't phony your way through golf. But, if it's something you are interested in anyway, it could be just the thing to put your career on the right trajectory.

6

Sales Rules

I have many sales rules that I have followed and that have stood me well throughout my career. I'd like to share them with you now.

Rule Number One: Don't let little obscure objections stop you from getting the sale. Do what you have to do to make the customer happy. Here's an example:

I once met with a company owner who had met with several of my competitors. He wanted about 25-30 phones, which was a nice sized order for me. One of my first questions to him at the meeting was, "Have you looked at other phone companies besides mine?"

He said, "Yes, about five companies."

When he said that, I replied, "Why haven't you bought a system already from one of my competitors?"

He said, "I want red phones. Everyone I met with has what I need, but no one can get me red phones."

I'm thinking to myself, no one makes red phones. Was I going to let that stop me at this moment from getting his order? Absolutely not.

I told him, "I can give you red phones with my system." He was pleasantly surprised to hear that, and based on that, I immediately asked him for the order. He signed the order on the spot. He wasn't kidding. That's what he wanted.

So now what do I do?

I called around to my supplier and found out I could get the phones spray painted. So that's what I did.

What if I couldn't get the phones spray painted red? I would have called the customer back and told him I couldn't get red phones. Then I would have moved on. In getting the order, was I lying? No! I would not let a detail stop me at that moment. What harm did I do by taking a chance? None!

Remember, don't let small details throw you off. Don't be too quick to say no before you've exhausted all possibilities. Remember, you're not a monopoly.

Rule Number Two: Know your decision maker; use psychology to lead the way. even if you use the "power lunch" method of getting a sale.

I met with a potential customer called Prestiege Window Manufacturing in Raritan. I got him to like me on the first meeting. At the second meeting, we came back with numbers and a contract for a $100,000 order. At his office to go over numbers, he suggested we go to lunch.

The meeting consisted of the owner, his junior partner, the controller, myself, and my son Damon. We went to an upscale Italian restaurant in Woodridge. Damon and I were alone in my car. I advised Damon to watch me follow the customer's lead at the luncheon. The customer ordered a double vodka. He looked over to me and asked what I was having, so I ordered the same as he was. Joel, the president of the company, was a definite power boss. We are all sitting there eating lunch, and we both ordered another one.

The controller, Sam, unexpectedly told me they weren't planning on making any decisions today because they were evaluating other systems and had other people coming in. Sam said, "Mike, we don't know if this system is exactly what we want. We will be looking at other systems and various companies to consider. So no decision will be made today."

I answered, "I can appreciate that, Sam, but I know this is the right system for your company." With that, I looked at Joel and repeated to him that no matter how he felt, Sam, his underling, said there would be no order placed today, in no uncertain terms.

Because I used reverse psychology on the power boss, challenging his authority, he said, "Mike, I'll do what I want."

"What is it that you want?" I asked.

"I want the system. Write it up, I'll sign it right here."

By using reverse psychology on Joel, knowing he was a

power boss, I knew his response would be that he would do what he wanted to do. A brilliant sales tactic.

My son Damon was in awe of what had just taken place.

The next day, in my office, I called Damon in and then called Joel, with Damon listening, to ask if Joel had buyer's remorse. He said no, not at all.

I didn't have to make that call, but I did it because it was the right thing to do. I knew the alcohol was a factor, and I didn't want to get new business based upon that. My advice is, always do the right thing, even if it means losing some business. Don't let greed or selfishness blind you. Especially if alcohol is involved!

Rule Number Three: When in doubt, ask for the order. I once did a deal with a company located in Bergen County, NJ. At our third meeting, the company president, who I had met with previously alone, invited 10 of his staff to come into the conference room to listen to my presentation. I had never had a meeting like this before, where 10 people were invited in at the spur of the moment. I was somewhat nervous, but also excited by the opportunity. How should I d this, I thought? Open the meeting to questions? Talk and then open up the meeting to questions?

I decided, rather than me dominating the dialogue, I opened it up to the group immediately for questions. I asked each person individually, "What is important to you concerning a phone system?" Each one had a different take on it.

An hour later the discussion was done, and the questions were asked and answered. Everyone seemed satisfied. I could offer them everything they wanted, and I knew it at that moment.

The president then thanked me for coming in and said he'd get back to me at a later date regarding their decision.

I thought to myself, what can I do to not let this opportunity slip away? I knew there was no time than right now to ask for the order, but how could I do it professionally in front of all these people?

Rather than leave, like most salespeople would have done, I said, I'm not doing that. It doesn't feel right to let this go.

Brazenly, but with tact, I said to the president: "You have all your people here, so you must think this is important. I know what it cost you to do this today in terms of lost time and productivity. Can I make a suggestion? Can I wait in the lobby, and since you have everyone here, you can discuss it and make a decision right now?"

The president honored my request and said, "That's not a bad idea, Mike. Have a seat in the lobby."

I waited in the lobby for about 15-20 minutes when he personally came and got me to bring me back to the conference room. They were all sitting there stone faced.

"Did you see professionalism and confidence and guts that Mike has?" the president said to his group. "I want my staff to pay attention to what you did so they can do it, too." He then proceeded to sign my order. It was a sales tale I will never forget.

Hence the advice: When in doubt, ask for the order.

Rule Number Four: (A) Treat EVERYONE with the respect you would give a decision maker, even if they don't have the authority to give you the order. From the receptionist all the way up to the CEO, everyone deserves your respect. Truly be interested in them.

(B) If you take a meeting with someone else who is not the final decision maker, but has been assigned to do the legwork and will report back to the decision maker, here is my advice: treat them as if they are the decision maker throughout your process. At the final meeting, use words like this: "So, (Mary), I know you don't have the authority to place an order with me today. But, hypothetically, if you had the authority to do so today, would you place the order with me?" Then wait for her reply. You will now not be in the dark as to your chances. It will get back to the decision maker that you treated other people and her in their company with respect.

If it's not a positive response, chances are you will not be getting that order. That's important to prevent you from living in unfounded hope and dying in despair.

Rule Number Five: One of the most important elements of sales is your own mental state. I can remember the time right after my oldest son, Damon, was born. I was ecstatic! Every meeting I went to, my first words to the people I met were that I'd just had a baby boy. My exuberance came through, as well as my positive energy. The first five customers I met after Damon was born all bought from me after the first meeting. Hard to believe, but totally true. How you think and feel comes across in a nonverbal manner that's very powerful.

On the other side of that coin, there are times when you know you just don't have "it" that day, so maybe that's a day to do paperwork rather than going out to meet clients. You can't use that excuse too often, and you have to have discipline, even on the days when you don't feel your absolute best. But it's not always the worst idea to give yourself a little break. Which leads to an interesting topic that can result from too much giving yourself a break.

CHAPTER

7

It's Better to Give Than to Receive

ook, dry spells are going to happen. No one, no matter how good you are, or how consistent you are, can be "on" one hundred percent of the time, every day, week, month, year. But, the key is, you can't let a dry spell last. So here's what you can do. The very first thing you have to ask yourself during a dry spell is, Am I doing everything I can? Go back to the formula. If you can't get leads, give more leads to others. Good things usually happen from that. Here's a story I can share with you that if I wasn't writing it, it would be hard to believe:

I'm in a sales meeting with my group. We were talking about how to get leads, so here's what I did.

I asked someone to bring me the Yellow Pages phone

book (remember them?). I closed my eyes, opened the book, put my finger down on a page and told everyone that this was the company I would call. It turned out to be an office furniture company.

In front of my group, I called the company, said who I was, and said that I had great leads.

"Who is your top producer selling?" I asked. "I want to give that person the lead." With that, I gave him the lead of someone who was looking for office furniture. Now this company knows me. I have a contact.

A month later, Mitsubishi Electric calls me and wants me to come in for a phone system. I ended up selling Mitsubishi a $50,000 system, the first of its kind. If fact, they ended up training my people on how to use it.

I asked my contact at Mitsubishi Electric where he had gotten my name. Can you guess? That's right, it was from the office furniture company that I found randomly in the Yellow Pages. It really works!

Sometimes you just have to recognize that a dry spell is part of a normal cycle in life. Don't dwell on the negative. Just go back to work. Everything will be fine.

Here's an example of what I mean. One time I sold a big system and we didn't get paid. That's right, the client, a government entity, didn't pay us. Payroll was due, and I was only in business about a year. The purchase order was overdue to the equipment manufacturer, with no payment in sight.

Here's what I did. I took my sales manager with me to the diner. I thought it would be a good idea to sit for 10 minutes out of the office and figure out what to do.

We both came to the conclusion that there was nothing we could do at that exact point. It was a government sale, and the check would just come when it came. After we finished our coffee, we went to canvas a few commercial buildings across the street from the diner. I got a couple of appointments.

By doing this, we felt good about ourselves. We were working hard. What I learned from that is that it always helps to know that you've done everything you can. That's true success.

By the way, the big government check came through later that week.

When you hit a dry spell, ask yourself these questions: Am I working my process as hard as I can? Am I getting appointments? Am I asking for the order? Another way to get past a dry spell is to look at everyone, and I mean EVERYONE, as a potential client. Now, do I mean trying to sell to everyone you meet? No, not necessarily. But don't look down on someone because you think there is no way that person could ever help you. I always asked new people I met what they do for a living.

I never looked at people through a jaundiced eye—"He's only a (fill in the blank)." Everybody deserves respect. I have always tried to learn from anyone. Even the deli guy. If you show respect to everyone, you'll get it back. And you'll also get people to remember you when they hear of someone who needs what you sell.

A very important thing to help with dry spells is to join your peers in networking groups. It helps you in two ways: you can find someone to mentor you, and you can mentor others. It's all about helping each other out. That can be very helpful to you an the people you're networking with.

Now for the biggie. One of the most important things I learned to snap a dry spell is to role play with your peers.

I knew that in order to teach anybody new sales tricks, you had to do it in person at a formal meeting once a week every week, at the same time in a controlled environment like a conference room. And one of the best methods of teaching is role playing.

Role playing isn't easy, and many people don't want to do it. I had people crying at my sessions because of the pressure. But it's an absolute necessity. You have to let someone else see what you are doing, and coach you through what you might be doing wrong. You get better at sales when you role play. Even the good salespeople get better with role playing. Everyone learns from each other the things that work and the things that don't.

If you're in that tough spot, ask someone to role play with you. Don't shy away from it. Let them ask you the tough questions that a potential customer would ask you, so that you can have the right answers ready. If you're in the teaching role, use role playing with your team. They may hate it at the time, but they will thank you when their numbers go in the right direction.

I have always met tremendous resistance with role playing. People would do anything not to role play. But sometimes they needed to learn that there is a certain way to walk in, a certain place to sit in a sales situation. Body language is extremely critical, as well. Remember, you chose sales as an career. If you can't role play, then this isn't for you.

8

Hiring The Right People

O f all the occupations to hire, of all the positions in the company, BY FAR, sales is the heart of any business. You still need the whole body of the car, but sales is the engine. Without a sale, nothing else happens.

Sales is also the hardest position to fill. Over time, I tried many different things to hire salespeople. If you take sales that are based on salary, it's not as tough to find a candidate. The greater the salary for a sales position, the easier it is to find qualified people.

When you are seeking sales professionals in a small company like mine, sales is critical but you can't afford to pay heavy salaries. This is, by far, the biggest challenge.

Finding a top salesperson who became successful was always my greatest challenge.

When searching for a sales professional, my process was to post a job in newspaper or online. You ask for resume. Over the years, I found that most of them were not accurate. So the first thing was to eliminate any resumes where something was obviously amiss.

Then I had my knockouts, things that immediately made me say "no thanks," which are:

First is where you live. If you live too far away from the office, I'm not calling you. Location matters. How long before the commute starts to kill you?

Next: If you had more than three jobs in the last five years, you're out. However, if I saw someone was making a high salary, that might be worth a phone call. I would ask why they wanted to leave such a high salary. Many times, I could read whether they were lying or not.

Next is the resume. If it's not presented right or has a lot of mistakes, I'm not calling them.

Then I'd look at someone moving to this state from another state. Why are you moving? Moving to another state was a big concern. It all depended on why you were moving. For example, if someone is moving because their spouse has a new opportunity, that's a red flag to me. The other reason many gave was moving to my state to take care of elderly loved ones. To me, that was a knockout. I couldn't take the risk.

If they passed all that, next would come the interview. My interview was based upon likeability. I went by instinct. If I felt they were reasonably qualified, I'd take it to the next step. I would give them a homework assignment. I'd ask them to drop me a note as to what they thought of our interview. What interested them? What concerns might they have? If someone didn't do that, then I'd know they weren't interested. If they did it poorly, they didn't have their thoughts together.

The next step was to test them. I used different third-party smart tests for two things: IQ for verbal and math, and emotional for sales. The third-party site would call me and evaluate the interviewee. If the recommendation from the third-party company was positive, then I would call them back in and go over results of strengths and weaknesses. I always hoped they would ask me for the job, i.e., close the deal, without me offering it. If they asked for the position, I felt really good about them.

Another thing you need to be very careful of when hiring people is to be as sure as possible that they are trustworthy. And that's not easy, and sometimes not even possible.

I had a great bookkeeper for 25 years, but she retired because technology was changing, and she just didn't want to learn all the new things she needed to know to do the job well. So I had to replace her.

I hired another bookkeeper. She was very good, very smart. She gave me references, but I later came to find out that she had it all planned out with them to con me. She manipulated the whole situation to get a job with me. I didn't realize she had been arrested for stealing from others.

Here's what she did. She befriended everyone in the company. She got hold of my credit cards. She got caught at the bank trying to cash a pretty sizable check. At that point, Wells Fargo called and Damon answered. Once he heard from the bank, we started to look at accounts and found she took over $250,000. I had always had a great track record with my manufacturers, and now we were really in the hole with many of them because she had been stealing money that we thought was going to our manufacturers.

I was away when I this all came out. I told Damon to call the police, and tell them you found she was stealing. The cops came and took her out in handcuffs.

I went in front of the judge in Elizabeth when it was time for her sentencing. I told the judge, "If you give her a slap on the wrist, she will do it again. She has already done it to others, and now she's done it to me. She was taking money from the whole company. She was heartless, calculating, and ruthless. Please do the right thing, your honor."

The judge turned to her and said, "Did you hear what he said? I agree with him 100 percent."

The moral of this story is when it comes to dealing with money, you have to remember that the love of money is the root of all evil. People will do some pretty terrible things for money.

Before this woman came to our company, I had a trustworthy bookkeeper and I gave her carte blanche. Because she was so good, I got too trusting, and the next bookkeeper robbed me blind. You really have to be on top of your employees. Don't trust anybody. If you're a little diligent, you can catch someone.

So now I owe $250,000 to my manufacturers. I called

them, explained what happened, and I said, "I'm going to pay you back. I just need a little time. Give me some extensions." And then I went on a selling tear. And I ended up paying back every penny I owed.

CHAPTER

9

Faith And Business

I want to start by saying that I love God (Jesus Christ). I was raised Catholic and went to Catholic school until eighth grade.

I was a boy who looked at things in black and white. Either I believe something or I don't believe it. I prefer to be definitive. In Catholic school when I was a student, they used to teach us about spending an eternity in hell. To me that was a big deal. It curbed my appetite to do what I wanted. I wanted to break rules, but I had to ask myself if what I was going to do was worth spending eternity in hell.

I remember asking a question of the nuns one time. I said, if I die with a mortal sin on my soul will I spend eternity in hell? Their answer was as a Catholic, if you die with a mortal sin on your soul, you can go to purgatory and with the prayers of your family, you would spend time in purgatory and then go to heaven.

This was awesome news! Now I knew that I wasn't doomed forever! It gave me more leeway to do things that I probably shouldn't have been doing.

For a while, I used this "purgatory" attitude in my business. I wouldn't blatantly lie to a customer or an employee. I would stretch a truth, but not outright lie. If it became an issue where I had to lie to get a sale, I wouldn't do it. But one thing I would always do was live up to what I said. Being human, I may not have remembered saying something, but if you could prove to me that I said it, then I would always live up to what I said.

As my love of God grew and I started reading and studying scripture (the Bible), I found that the purgatory idea was a myth. There is no such thing as hell or purgatory. When you die, you either belong to Christ and go to heaven for eternity, or you don't. You no longer exist. The reward is eternal life. The penalty is non-existence. Is a few short years on this earth living the wrong way, worth giving up eternity in paradise with God? For me, no contest.

Here's an example: After I left Intertel, I couldn't get a manufacturer to sell me their products. I tried and tried and, unbelievably, I couldn't get a manufacturer to sell me their equipment. But guess who was there like a Chesire cat ready to pounce? My old friend, business partner, and nemesis, Mr. Wichansky. He said, "Mike, I'll sell you the equipment through Intertel. You won't be an official authorized dealer, but we'll give you dealer prices. But you will have to personally pay me a five percent vig (vigorish) on every sale for as long as you buy the Intertel equipment through me in my NJ/NY offices. Remember, I wasn't an authorized dealer. He flew in the CEO of Intertel. We met in a hotel lobby and I signed that agreement with the CEO's blessing and Mr. Wichansky's concurrence.

They were willing to do this because they thought I would sell their products, ultimately fail as an owner, come back to them with hat in hand, and they would pick up all the accounts that I killed myself to get anyway. To them it was a safe bet, and he would make five percent on my sales. They asked me at the meeting to arrange this deal, "Mike, do we have your word that you'll pay this forever?" I shook their hands and said yes. They knew that I was a man of my word. In my mind's eye, I'm now stuck between a rock and a hard place, but had no choice but to go through with it.

Unbelievably, I bought $1 million from Intertel wholesale in my first year in business. I became an accounting burden to them. It looked like they were losing money in their NY/NJ offices because of my wholesale purchases. They were a public company, and their books didn't reflect a profit.

Because of my success with the Intertel product, I got invited to a once-in-a-lifetime trip to South Korea to Samsung with the president of Intertel and all the top dealers in the country. One of the people on the trip happened to be the president of Sprint Corp., who was there looking at the product for his company to sell through their dealer network. This gentleman took a liking to me as we were there and learned of my status of not being an authorized dealer with that peculiar arrangement with Mr. Wichansky.

Intertel was going to sell their product to Sprint directly, and Sprint would have their own authorized dealers selling the Intertel product with the Sprint name. The president of Sprint said he wanted Mike Finaldi (Tele-Solutions) to become an authorized dealer of the product through Sprint Corp. The CEO of Intertel said no, you can't have him. Sprint refused to make a deal without me and my company representing them. Sprint was willing to walk away from a nation-wide multi-million dollar contract because of little ole me. If this wasn't true, isn't it a little hard to believe? Believe it, because I became the number one authorized Sprint dealer in the country for many years. I no longer had to pay him his five percent vig. I'm ecstatic.

I conducted my business with my belief in God in mind. I had faith that things would work out okay for me. I never worked on the premise of how much I could get away with, but rather one of not hurting anybody. I went by my heart. I wasn't out to cheat or hurt anyone. Sometimes, even if I saw that I could win, if I thought it was detrimental, I would lose just so it wouldn't hurt another person. I could never tolerate injustice.

My career took its course because of opposition and injustice. I didn't get promoted at Bell because of what I perceived as injustice. My lack of knowledge of the buyout at TCI—another injustice. But I always knew God was looking out for me. I always trusted that He would do the right thing for me. Here's a prime example of that.

I have three children. The first two were born as healthy

as could be, and everything was great. Then, along came my third child, my son Vincent.

When Vincent was born, he had a non-functioning adrenal gland. We were afraid he was going to die. The doctors informed me that if he lived, he would need hormones which would cause stunted growth and other severe medical issues for the rest of his life. I can't imagine anything scarier for a parent than that. I can't even tell you how I felt.

So what did I do? I prayed. I talked to God. I asked him to take me instead of Vincent. I told myself that I would change my life if God would save my son.

After I made my peace with God, the next day the doctors incredulously told me, "Mr. Finaldi, we don't understand what just took place. We see no medical evidence that this ever happened." They were stunned. They then told me they were writing about his case for the *New England Medical Journal*.

From that day on, my relationship with God has grown and grown. I read scripture every day.

Vincent is still here, married to Lisa and is the proud father of a beautiful son named Leo.

As of the writing of this book, my beautiful daughter Cara is married to John, with three children, Michael, Gabriella, and Gianna.

Damon, my oldest, is married to Faye with four children: Matthew, Maria, Dean, and Gabe.

You could say that God has had my back and Lorraine's, and blessed us many times over.

10

Working With Family

M y business was mine, and mine alone, for many years. I loved the challenge of it. Eventually my children got older. The possibility always existed in my mind of being able to hand the business over to my kids someday, especially as I got older. But thinking about it and actually doing it are two entirely different things.

First, a little background:

My oldest son, Damon, graduated from Penn State in 1999. He was an industrial engineer and worked for Price Waterhouse in New York City. He was working there but flying all over the country. Then 9/11 happened, and of course, this changed his outlook on traveling so much, as well as mine concerning him.

At this same time, I saw the telecommunications industry was strong and becoming much more technical than it ever had been. I also wanted an exit strategy. I knew I would want to get out eventually and retire. I could have sold the business for good money, but then, as far as my family went, it would end. I wanted to give the kids the opportunity to grow the business.

I called Damon and told him I was planning to sell the business in the next year or two. However, I also told him that I would be willing to not to sell it if he wanted to come in and I would teach him everything I knew about business, sales, and entrepreneurship. He would see it all.

I told him to sleep on it. I let him know that if he decided not to come in, I wouldn't be mad at him at all, and he wouldn't disappoint me.

A couple of days later he said yes, and we took it from there. The early days were easier because he didn't know anything. More on that to come.

My daughter Cara was next. She graduated from Quinnipiac with a degree in social work. She came into the business right after college on the service side. Cara really wanted the comfort of a family-owned business. She got involved in service department as a customer liaison dispatcher. She was, and still is, very good at her job. She's a very caring person.

Now I had an agenda. Damon's talents were more on the technical sales side. He's an organization guy. He's great with flow charts, money flow, etc. Damon worries about the minutae. So now I had him to organize, and Cara to work with the service team. Things were going well.

And then came Vincent. Being the baby of the family, he was somewhat coddled. I knew he wasn't ready right out of college. He was a marketing major. Now I really wanted him to come in. I was being a little selfish. I didn't want to wait for him to have a year or two in the private sector and then come to Tele-Solutions.

I knew I had a successful business. I knew Vincent would do well. And it was getting to be time; I wanted to get out. This was around 2004 or 2005. I knew I would have to teach Vincent for more than a few years. I wanted to be out when I was 62 or 63. So in came Vincent, and now I orchestrated to have the whole crew working there.

That's when I had to learn humility. They were my children. I was used to being the captain, but when my kids came in it was different. I didn't want to win by power. They made some decisions I didn't agree with. And if it was anyone else but my kids, I could rule with an iron fist. But you have to be so much more careful with family. You still want them to come over for Sunday dinner and bring the grandkids to see you. You can have your way in the office, but will that ruin the whole family dynamic? Yes. Is that worth it? In my eyes, definitely not. That being said, swallowing things wasn't always easy.

Years later, we're at the point where Damon and Vincent want control of Tele-Solutions, because of my earlier promise. Around 2013 or so, I called in our family accountant, Vincent and Damon, Unfortunately, I didn't have Cara or Lorraine attend the meeting. I didn't think it was necessary. That was a mistake. In looking back on it, I wish they had joined us that day to see what my true intentions were for the family.

In the end, what I planned, which did work out, was to create a business and turn over control to my family. Now it's their turn to take it to the next level. They now have a thriving business they can call their own and turn over to their kids if they desire.

While we are discussing family, here's another piece of advice: be very careful of who you marry. Besides your relationship with God (if you have one), the next most important relationship in your life is with your spouse. Divorce affects everyone in your family and everything in your life, both personal and professional. Choose wisely.

Words To Live By

Just like my sales rules from an earlier chapter, I have many motivational quotes that have helped me through my career and my everyday living. Let me share them with you now.

Don't live in hope and die in despair. This taught me to be realistic about my prospects of actually getting an order. I would go over my checklist and play a movie in my mind of the meetings I had with this particular prospect. I would then plan a course of action needed or required to bring it home. It helped me through some of the toughest sales I've ever made. It also taught me to be realistic about my life.

On time all the time as promised. I was always prompt and courteous. I would follow up always before I actually left for the appointment. Most of the time with the decision maker, I would call directly before I drove to his office, even if I had already called to confirm the day before. I did not want to waste my time and feel bad about myself if I was stood up. It was hard to recover from stupidity if I drove out to a prospect's place of business and they weren't there.

If I was afraid that they might cancel, I followed up my agreed-upon appointment with a particular big decision maker. I would ask for his secretary, not him, and confirm that he was in without talking to him directly. It's hard for him to not see me if I came to his office and he was there. I'm calling to confirm and instead of asking, I just call to say I'm confirming. I didn't want to go out there and have them blow me off; then I've wasted my time and I feel bad about myself. Time is money. I tend to be like this in everyday life. If I say I'll be there, it's very rare that I'm not. You can always count on me.

Faint heart never won fair lady. This one I used as motivation to make a call to a prospect if I was feeling tentative and reluctant to do it. I thought about it and then did it. You have to go after what you want. It won't just come to you.

People don't change that much. You can't put in what God left out. It's hard enough to get out what God left in. This has to do with sales talent. It refers mostly to salespeople that I was training. It really refers to any job that requires a skill. As a manager, it's important to be realistic with employees that are working under your supervision and guidance, as well as yourself. The takeaway is don't waste your time and effort if it's unrealistic for a person to succeed.

This motto pertains in both business and life. You have to be realistic about who a person really is in everyday life and relationships as well as in business. **Stay away from SNIOPs (Susceptible to negative influence of people)** This is very important to live by in life, regardless of type of occupation. This pertains to everyone who wants to be happy, positive and upbeat. Life at times can be hard. No one needs unfounded negativity from others. If you tell someone how you feel about this, and they continue their negativity, stop seeing them. Life is too short for negativity. It's easier for people to complain than it is to do something about their situation or circumstances. Don't let them bring you down! Friends, family, business associates...the whole shooting match. It's easier to become negative than it is to be positive. Knowing that, you must surround yourself as much as possible with positive people and input.

Be strong and of good courage. Trust in the Lord with all thy heart and lean not on your own understanding. This is my favorite scripture that I say often. Things happen in life that are out of our control. I use this Scripture all the time knowing that God is in charge and I leave it at that.

If it doesn't feel good, it's not good. This is a matter of simple trust in your inner self and feelings. It's not cerebral. It's not meant to debate or rationalize. Your inner self, if you are grounded properly, is telling you something. Trust it. This motto is profound.

And this final one, I believe, is self-explanatory:

Tell me, I forget; show me, I remember; involve me, I understand.

So, in conclusion, I hope these stories, these sales ideas, help you in your path of what you do in your life. But most of all follow your heart, it's never wrong.

God bless, have fun, do well.

Printed in the United States
By Bookmasters